ANTIETAM

National Battlefield Site · Maryland

by Frederick Tilberg

NATIONAL PARK SERVICE HISTORICAL HANDBOOK SERIES NO. 31

Washington, D.C. · 1960

(Revised 1961)

The National Park System, of which Antietam National Battlefield Site is a unit, is dedicated to conserving the scenic, scientific, and historic heritage of the United States for the benefit and inspiration of its people.

ANTIETAM

National Battlefield Site - Maryland

By Frederick Tilberg

Digital Scanning and Publishing is a leader in the electronic republication of historical books and documents. We publish many of our titles as eBooks, paperback and hardcover editions. DSI is committed to bringing many traditional and well-known books back to life, retaining the look and feel of the original work.

Trade Paperback ISBN: 1-58218-782-7

©2010 DSI Digital Reproduction
First DSI Printing: May 2010

Published by Digital Scanning Inc. Scituate, MA 02066 781-545-2100 http://www.Digitalscanning.com and http://www.PDFLibrary.com

Contents

I N WESTERN MARYLAND *is a stream called Antietam Creek. Nearby is the quiet town of Sharpsburg. The scene is pastoral, with rolling hills and farmlands and patches of woods. Stone monuments and bronze tablets dot the landscape. They seem strangely out of place. Only some extraordinary event can explain their presence.*

Almost by chance, two great armies collided here. Gen. Robert E. Lee's Army of Northern Virginia was invading the North. Maj. Gen. George B. McClellan's Army of the Potomac was out to stop him. On September 17, 1862—the bloodiest day of the Civil War—the two armies fought the Battle of Antietam to decide the issue.

Their violent conflict shattered the quiet of Maryland's countryside. When the hot September sun finally set upon the devastated battlefield, 23,000 Americans had fallen—nearly eight times more than fell on Tarawa's beaches in World War II. This single fact, with the heroism and suffering it implies, gives the monuments and markers their meaning. No longer do they presume upon the land. Rather, their mute inadequacy can only hint of the great event that happened here—and of its even greater consequences.

Across the Potomac

On September 5–6, 1862, a ragged host of nearly 55,000 men in butternut and gray splashed across the Potomac River at White's Ford near Leesburg, Va. This was Gen. Robert E. Lee's Army of North-

Focal point of the early morning attacks, the Dunkard Church and some who defended it. From photograph attributed to James Gardner. Courtesy, Library of Congress.

ern Virginia embarked on the Confederacy's first invasion of the North. Though thousands of Lee's men were shoeless, though they lacked ammunition and supplies, though they were fatigued from the marching and fighting just before the historic crossing into Maryland, they felt invincible.

Only a week before, August 28–30, they had routed the Federals at the Battle of Second Manassas, driving them headlong into the defenses of Washington. With this event, the strategic initiative so long held by Union forces in the East had shifted to the Confederacy. But Lee recognized that Union power was almost limitless. It must be kept off balance—prevented from reorganizing for another drive on Richmond, the Confederate capital. Only a sharp offensive thrust by Southern arms would do this.

Because his army lacked the strength to assault Washington, General Lee had decided on September 3 to invade Maryland. North of the Potomac his army would be a constant threat to Washington. This would keep Federal forces out of Virginia, allowing that ravaged land to recuperate from the campaigning that had stripped it. It would give Maryland's people, many of whom sympathized with the South, a chance to throw off the Northern yoke.

From Maryland, Lee could march into Pennsylvania, disrupting the east-west rail communications of the North, carrying the brunt of war into that rich land, drawing on its wealth to refit his army.

Lee's army crossing the Potomac; Union scouts in foreground. From wartime sketch by A. R. Waud. Courtesy, Library of Congress.

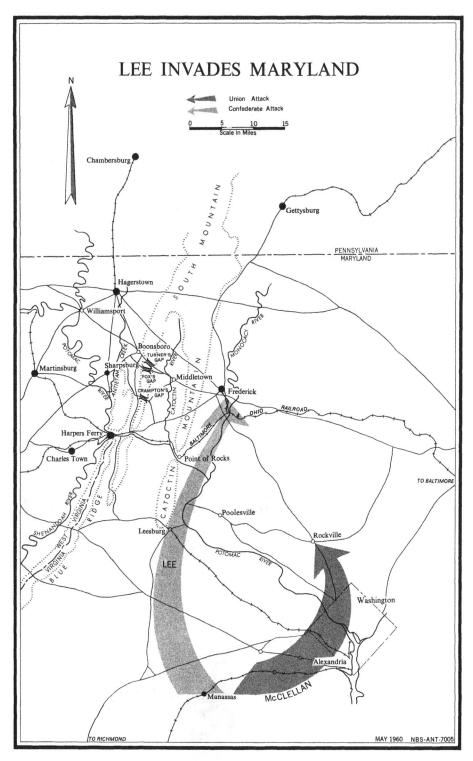

LEE INVADES MARYLAND

N

Union Attack
Confederate Attack

0   5   10   15
Scale in Miles

Chambersburg

Gettysburg

PENNSYLVANIA
MARYLAND

SOUTH MOUNTAIN

Hagerstown

Williamsport

POTOMAC

MONOCACY RIVER

Boonsboro
TURNER'S GAP

Martinsburg

Sharpsburg

ANTIETAM CREEK

FOX'S GAP

CRAMPTON'S GAP

Middletown

CATOCTIN MOUNTAIN

Frederick

OHIO RAILROAD

BALTIMORE

Harpers Ferry

Charles Town

Point of Rocks

TO BALTIMORE

CATOCTIN

SHENANDOAH RIVER

VIRGINIA

WEST VIRGINIA

BLUE RIDGE

Poolesville

Leesburg

LEE

POTOMAC RIVER

Rockville

Washington

Alexandria

Manassas

McCLELLAN

TO RICHMOND

Larger political possibilities loomed, too. The North was war weary. If, in the heartland of the Union, Lee could inflict a serious defeat on Northern arms, the Confederacy might hope for more than military dividends—the result might be a negotiated peace on the basis of Southern independence. Too, a successful campaign might induce England and France to recognize the Confederacy and to intervene for the purpose of mediating the conflict.

So it was that the hopes of the South rode with this Army of Northern Virginia as it marched into Frederick, Md., on September 7.

McClellan in Command

On that same September 7, another army assembled at Rockville, Md., just northwest of Washington. Soon to be nearly 90,000 strong, this was Maj. Gen. George B. McClellan's Army of the Potomac. Its goal: To stay between Lee's army and Washington, to seek out the Confederate force, and, as President Abraham Lincoln hoped, to destroy it.

Hastily thrown together to meet the challenge of Lee's invasion, this Union army was a conglomerate of all the forces in the Washington vicinity. Some of its men were fresh from the recruiting depots— they lacked training and were deficient in arms. Others had just returned from the Peninsular Campaign where Lee's army had driven them from the gates of Richmond in the Seven Days' Battles, June 26–July 2. Still others were the remnants of the force so decisively beaten at Second Manassas.

Gen. Robert E. Lee. From photograph by Julian Vannerson. Courtesy, Library of Congress.

Maj. Gen. George B. McClellan.
From photograph by Matthew B. Brady
or assistant. Courtesy, National Archives.

In McClellan the Union army had a commander who was skilled at organization. This was the reason President Lincoln and Commander in Chief of the Army Henry Halleck had chosen him for command on September 3. In 4 days he had pulled together this new army and had gotten it on the march. It was a remarkable achievement.

But in other respects, McClellan was the object of doubt. He was cautious. He seemed to lack that capacity for full and violent commitment essential to victory. Against Lee, whose blood roused at the sound of the guns, McClellan's methodical nature had once before proved wanting—during the Seven Days' Battles. At least so thought President Lincoln.

But this time McClellan had started well. Could he now catch Lee's army and destroy it, bringing the end of the war in sight? Or, failing that, could he at least gain a favorable decision? A victory in the field would give the President a chance to issue the Emancipation Proclamation, which he had been holding since midsummer. The proclamation would declare free the slaves in the Confederate States. By this means, Lincoln hoped to infuse the Northern cause with regenerative moral power. Spirits were lagging in the North. Unless a moral purpose could be added to the North's primary war aim of restoring the Union, Lincoln questioned whether the will to fight could be maintained in the face of growing casualty lists.

And so, followed by mingled doubt and hope, McClellan started in pursuit of the Confederate army. McClellan himself was aware of these mingled feelings. He knew that Lincoln and Halleck had come to him as a last resort in a time of emergency. He knew they doubted his energy and ability as a combat commander. Even his orders were unclear, for they did not explicitly give him authority to pursue the enemy beyond the defenses of Washington.

Burdened with knowledge of this lack of faith, wary of taking risks because of his ambiguous orders, McClellan marched toward his encounter with the victorious and confident Lee.

Lee Divides His Forces

Maryland was a disappointment to Lee. On September 8, he had issued a dignified proclamation inviting the men of that State to join his command and help restore Maryland to her rightful place among the Southern States. His words concluded with assurance that the Marylanders could make their choice with no fear of intimidation from the victorious Confederate army in their midst.

Maryland took him at his word. Her people did not flock to the Confederate standard, nor were they much help in provisioning his army. No doubt Lee's barefooted soldiers were a portent to

First Virginia Cavalry at a halt during invasion of Maryland. From wartime sketch by Waud. Courtesy, Library of Congress.

these people, who had previously seen only well-fed, well-equipped Federal troops.

Deprived of expected aid, Lee had to move onward to Pennsylvania quickly. For one thing, unless he could get shoes for his men, his army might melt away. Straggling was already a serious problem, for Maryland's hard roads tortured bare feet toughened only to the dirt lanes of Virginia.

By now, Lee's scouts were bringing reports of the great Federal army slowly pushing out from Rockville toward Frederick.

Lee's proposed route into Pennsylvania was dictated by geography. West of Frederick—beyond South Mountain—is the Cumberland Valley. This is the northern half of the Great Valley that sweeps northeastward through Virginia, Maryland, and Pennsylvania. That part of the Great Valley immediately south of the Potomac is called the Shenandoah Valley.

Lee planned to concentrate his army west of the mountains near Hagerstown, Md. There he would be in direct line with his supply base at Winchester in the Shenandoah Valley. After replenishing his supplies and ammunition, he could strike northeast through the Cumberland Valley toward Harrisburg, Pa., where he could destroy the Pennsylvania Railroad bridge across the Susquehanna River. Once loose in the middle of Pennsylvania he could live off the country and threaten Philadelphia, Baltimore, and Washington.

Before launching this daring maneuver, Lee must first clear his line of communications through the Shenandoah Valley to Winchester and to Richmond. Blocking it were strong Federal garrisons at Harpers Ferry and Martinsburg. Unaccountably, they had remained at their posts after the Confederate army crossed the Potomac. Now they must be cleared out.

Lee decided to accomplish this mission by boldly dividing his army into four parts. On September 9, he issued Special Order 191. Briefly, it directed Maj. Gen. James Longstreet and Maj. Gen. D. H. Hill to proceed across South Mountain toward Boonsboro and Hagerstown. Three columns cooperating under Maj. Gen. Thomas J. "Stonewall" Jackson were ordered to converge on Harpers Ferry from the northwest, northeast, and east. En route, the column under Jackson's immediate command was to swing westward and catch any Federals remaining at Martinsburg. Maj. Gen. Lafayette McLaws, approaching from the northeast, was to occupy Maryland Heights, which overlooks Harpers Ferry from the north side of the Potomac. Brig. Gen. John Walker, approaching from the east, was to occupy Loudoun Heights, across the Shenandoah River from Harpers Ferry. Maj. Gen. J. E. B. Stuart's cavalry was to screen these movements from McClellan by remaining east of South Mountain.

(At this point a fateful event occurred—one which was destined to change the subsequent course of the campaign. D. H. Hill, Jackson's

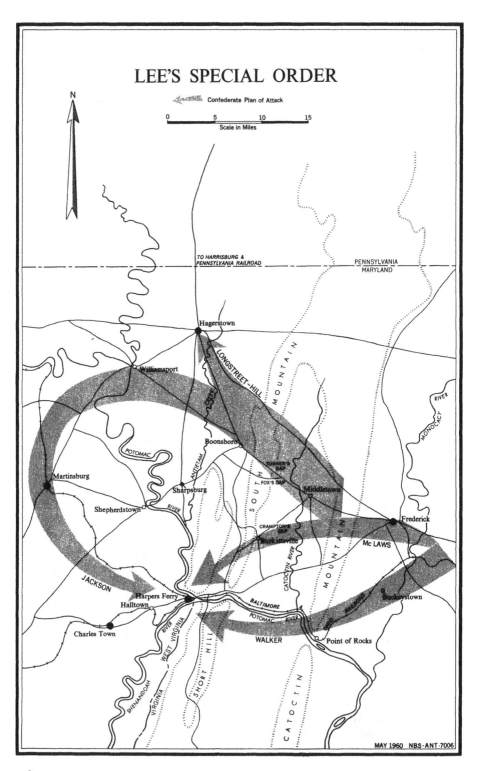

LEE'S SPECIAL ORDER

Confederate Plan of Attack

0 ___ 5 ___ 10 ___ 15
Scale in Miles

N

TO HARRISBURG &
PENNSYLVANIA RAILROAD

PENNSYLVANIA
MARYLAND

Hagerstown

Williamsport

LONGSTREET-HILL

Boonsboro

POTOMAC

ANTIETAM

Martinsburg

Sharpsburg

Shepherdstown

RIVER

SOUTH MOUNTAIN

TURNER'S GAP

FOX'S GAP

CRAMPTON'S GAP

Middletown

Frederick

Mc LAWS

MONOCACY

RIVER

Burkittsville

CATOCTIN RIVER

JACKSON

Harpers Ferry

Halltown

Charles Town

SHENANDOAH

VIRGINIA

WEST VIRGINIA

SHORT HILL

BALTIMORE

POTOMAC

RIVER

WALKER

Point of Rocks

Buckeystown

CATOCTIN MOUNTAIN

MAY 1960 NBS-ANT-7006

8

brother-in-law, had until this time been under Jackson's command. Unaware that a copy of Lee's order had already been sent to Hill, Jackson now prepared an extra copy for that officer. Hill kept the copy from Jackson; the other was to provide the script for much of the drama that followed.)

Lee was courting danger by thus dividing his force in the face of McClellan's advancing army. Against a driving opponent, Lee probably would not have done it. But he felt certain that McClellan's caution would give Jackson the margin of time needed to capture Harpers Ferry and reunite with Longstreet before the Federal army could come within striking distance. That margin was calculated at 3 or 4 days. By September 12, Jackson's force should be marching north toward Hagerstown. As soon as the army reconcentrated there, Lee could begin his dash up the Cumberland Valley into Pennsylvania.

So confident was Lee of the marching capacities of the Harpers Ferry columns, and so certain was he that McClellan would approach slowly, that he made no provision for guarding the gaps through South Mountain.

The Lost Order

Lee's army departed Frederick on September 10. Two days later leading elements of McClellan's army entered that city. On September 13, came McClellan himself with his usual cavalcade of staff officers.

Maj. Gen. James Longstreet. Courtesy, Library of Congress.

Maj. Gen. Thomas J. "Stonewall" Jackson. From photograph by George W. Minnes. Courtesy, Library of Congress.

That same afternoon a copy of Lee's Special Order 191 was discovered in the encampment grounds previously used by the Confederate army. Quickly it was passed to McClellan. The handwriting was recognized as that of Col. R. H. Chilton, Lee's assistant adjutant general; the document's authenticity could not be doubted.

The fate of Lee's army literally lay in McClellan's hands. If he slashed swiftly through the South Mountain gaps and planted his army squarely between Longstreet's force near Hagerstown and Jackson's columns at Harpers Ferry, he could overwhelm the Confederate detachments in turn.

But again McClellan was methodical. Not until the next morning, September 14, did his heavy columns get underway. This crucial delay was to give Lee the chance to pull his army together at the small town of Sharpsburg.

Fighting for Time at South Mountain

By September 12, Lee had begun to worry. Stuart's scouts had reported the Federal approach to Frederick. McClellan was moving too fast. Next evening things looked worse. Jackson had not yet captured Harpers Ferry, and already McClellan's forward troops were pushing Stuart back toward the South Mountain gaps. Delay at Harpers Ferry made these passes through South Mountain the key to the situation. They must be defended.

South Mountain is the watershed between the Middletown and

The Battle of South Mountain. From lithograph by Endicott. Courtesy, Library of Congress.

Cumberland Valleys. The Frederick-Hagerstown road leads through Middletown, then goes over South Mountain at Turner's Gap. At the eastern base of the mountain, the old road to Sharpsburg turned south from the main road and passed through Fox's Gap, a mile south of Turner's Gap. Four miles farther south is Crampton's Gap, reached by another road from Middletown.

On the night of September 13, Lee ordered all available forces to defend these three passes. D. H. Hill, with Longstreet coming to his aid, covered Turner's and Fox's Gaps. McLaws sent part of his force back from Maryland Heights to hold Crampton's Gap.

Next morning the thin-stretched Confederate defenders saw McClellan's powerful columns marching across Middletown Valley. Up the roads to the gaps they came—ponderous and inexorable. The right wing of McClellan's army under Maj. Gen. Ambrose Burnside assaulted Turner's and Fox's Gaps. The left wing under Maj. Gen. William Franklin struck through Crampton's Gap. By nightfall, September 14, the superior Federal forces had broken through at Crampton's Gap; and Burnside's men were close to victory at the northern passes. The way to the valley was open.

By his stubborn defense at South Mountain, Lee had gained a day. But was it enough? McClellan's speed and shrewd pursuit, together with Jackson's inability to meet the demanding schedule set forth in Special Order 191, had fallen upon Lee with all the weight of a strategic surprise. No longer could he command events, pick his own objectives, and make the Federal army conform to his moves. Rather, the decision at South Mountain had snatched the initiative away from Lee. His plan for an offensive foray into Pennsylvania was wrecked. Now it was a question of saving his army.

The first step was to call off the attack on Harpers Ferry. At 8 p.m., September 14, Lee sent a dispatch to McLaws stating,

Harpers Ferry looking east toward confluence of Potomac and Shenandoah Rivers. Ruins of armory in right foreground. Maryland Heights, left; Loudoun Heights, right. From 1862 photograph by Brady. Courtesy, Library of Congress.

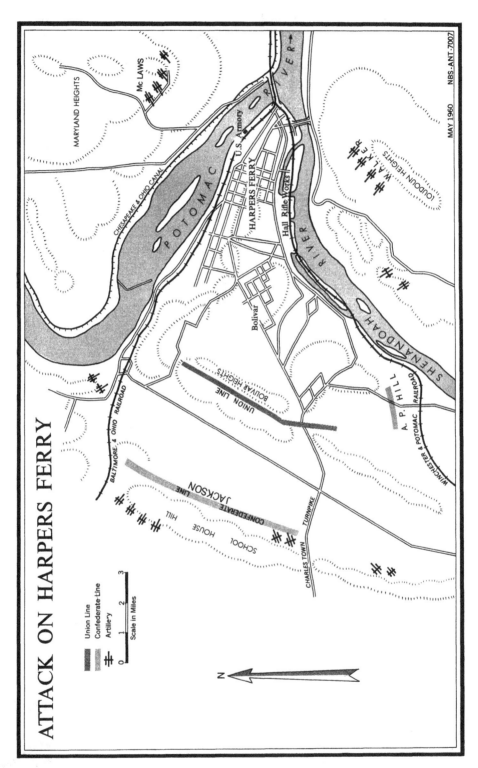

ATTACK ON HARPERS FERRY

MARYLAND HEIGHTS

Mc LAWS

CHESAPEAKE & OHIO CANAL

POTOMAC RIVER

U.S. Armory

HARPERS FERRY

Hall Rifle Works

LOUDOUN HEIGHTS

A. P. HILL

SHENANDOAH RIVER

Bolivar

BALTIMORE & OHIO RAILROAD

UNION LINE

BOLIVAR HEIGHTS

JACKSON

CONFEDERATE LINE

SCHOOL HOUSE HILL

CHARLES TOWN TURNPIKE

WINCHESTER & POTOMAC RAILROAD

Union Line
Confederate Line
Artillery

0 1 2 3
Scale in Miles

N

MAY 1960   NBS-ANT-7007

The day has gone against us and this army will go by Sharpsburg and cross the river. It is necessary for you to abandon your position tonight. . . . Send forward officers to explore the way, ascertain the best crossing of the Potomac, and if you can find any between you and Shepherdstown leave Shepherdstown Ford for this command." Jackson was ordered ". . . to take position at Shepherdstown to cover Lee's crossing into Virginia."

But then came a message from Jackson: Harpers Ferry was about to fall. Perhaps there was still hope. If Jackson could capture Harpers Ferry early the next day, the army could reunite at Sharpsburg. Good defensive ground was there; a victory over McClellan might enable Lee to continue his campaign of maneuver; and should disaster threaten, the fords of the Potomac were nearby.

At 11:15 p.m., Lee countermanded his earlier order; the attack on Harpers Ferry was to proceed. Shortly after, Longstreet's divisions began to march through the night toward Sharpsburg.

Harpers Ferry Surrenders

The village of Harpers Ferry lies at the gateway cut through the mountains by the Potomac and Shenandoah Rivers, whose waters join there. Situated at the apex of the triangle of land between the rivers, the town is completely dominated by Loudoun and Maryland Heights. By nightfall of September 14, McLaws and Walker had artillery on these heights ready for plunging fire into the town; Jackson had stretched his lines across the base of the triangle between the rivers.

Caught in this trap were nearly 12,000 Federal troops commanded by Col. D. S. Miles. Their position was indefensible.

At daybreak on September 15, the surrounding Confederate artillery opened fire. At 8 a.m., the hopelessness of his position confirmed, Miles ordered the surrender; he was killed in the last moments of the battle.

Jackson immediately sent word of his victory to Lee. Then, after assigning Maj. Gen. A. P. Hill's division to dispose of prisoners and booty, he prepared the rest of his troops for the hard march ahead.

The same dawn that signaled Jackson's guns to open fire on Harpers Ferry revealed Longstreet's tired soldiers taking position on the rolling hills around Sharpsburg. As he watched them, Lee still did not know whether to fight or to withdraw across the Potomac. Decision waited upon word from Jackson. The word came; it was good; the crisis was past. Even now Lee's messenger hurried to direct Jackson's veterans toward Sharpsburg. Confident that the entire army would soon be at hand, certain that he could whip McClellan, Lee decided to fight.

Sharpsburg shortly after the Battle of Antietam. Taken from crest of Sharpsburg Ridge, looking west down Boonsboro Pike toward Potomac River. Hagerstown Pike heads north (right) just beyond large tree in left-center. Lee's headquarters were in Oak Grove in distance, just to right of Boonsboro Pike.

Lee Takes a Stand on Sharpsburg Ridge

Lee's decision to make his stand on the low ridge extending north and south of Sharpsburg might well have led to disaster for the Confederate army. A large part of his force was still scattered and several miles away. Backed against the coils of the Potomac River, with only the ford near Shepherdstown offering an avenue of withdrawal, a reversal in battle could result in rout and consequent loss of thousands of men and scores of guns. Longstreet voiced disapproval of battle at Sharpsburg. Jackson, hurriedly examining the ground on his arrival from Harpers Ferry, strongly favored Lee's choice.

The village of Sharpsburg lies in a small valley at the western base of Sharpsburg Ridge. From the village, the Boonsboro Pike leads east across the ridge, then across Antietam Creek. The Hagerstown Pike extends northward on the crest of the ridge.

From the Hagerstown Pike, gently rolling farmland spreads a mile eastward to Antietam Creek and the same distance westward to the winding Potomac River. A mile north of Sharpsburg was a heavy patch of trees known as West Woods; it was about 300 yards wide at its southern limits, tapering to 200 yards or less as it stretched away northwest from the pike. Half a mile east of Hagerstown Pike was another patch of trees called East Woods; it was 200 yards wide and extended a quarter mile south across the Smoketown Road. North Woods, a triangular plot of trees, stretched east from the Hagerstown Pike over the Poffenberger farm. Half a mile to the west looms Nicodemus Hill, a prominent landmark near the Potomac. Artillery on its heights would command the open ground lying between the patches of woodland. In this open area east of the Hagerstown Pike lay a 40-acre cornfield. West of the pike were outcroppings of rock running nearly parallel to the road—ready-made fortifications. Adjacent to the Hagerstown Pike, on a slight rise near the lower end of West Woods, stood a Dunkard Church, a small white building framed by massive oaks. Southeast of Sharpsburg, rolling land broken by deep ravines extends a mile beyond to a sharp bend in Antietam Creek.

Crossings of swiftly flowing Antietam Creek were readily available. The road extending northwest from Keedysville went over the stream at the Upper Bridge, the road to Sharpsburg from Boonsboro over the Middle Bridge, and the road to Sharpsburg from Pleasant Valley over the Lower Bridge. The stream could be crossed, also, at Pry's Mill Ford, a half mile south of the Upper Bridge, at Snavely's Ford, nearly a mile south of the Lower Bridge, and at other unnamed fording places.

With its advantages of woodland and outcroppings of rock ledges, Lee believed that the ridge north of Sharpsburg offered a strong battle position. Though he had ample time to construct earthworks, the Confederate commander chose to rely wholly on natural defenses.

As Lee's men approached from Boonsboro during the morning hours of September 15, they turned left and right off the pike to form their lines on Sharpsburg Ridge. Brig. Gen. John Hood, with only two brigades, held the ground at the fringe of the West Woods—from the Dunkard Church northwest to Nicodemus Hill near the Potomac. Here, Stuart's cavalry protected the left end or flank of the line. From Hood's position southward to Sharpsburg, D. H. Hill placed his five brigades east of and paralleling the Hagerstown Pike. Brig. Gen. Nathan Evan's brigade occupied the center of the line in front of Sharpsburg; his men straddled the Boonsboro Pike. The six brigades of Maj. Gen. D. R. Jones extended the Confederate front southeast nearly a mile to the Lower Bridge over Antietam Creek. The fords over the Antietam at the extreme right of the line were guarded by Col. Thomas Munford's cavalry brigade. Artillery was placed at vantage points on the ridges.

Throughout the 15th, Lee presented a show of strength with 14 brigades of infantry and 3 of cavalry—about 18,000 men.

Army supply train crosses Middle Bridge over Antietam Creek. After ascent of ridge in background, Boonsboro Pike dips into a ravine, then ascends Sharpsburg Ridge and enters the village. Courtesy, National Archives.

McClellan Concentrates at the Antietam

Against this pretense of power, General McClellan marched cautiously on the forenoon of the 15th, over good roads and in fine weather. By noon, he arrived at the Confederate front with a force of nearly 75,000 men. McClellan hesitated, and the day wore away.

As the early morning fog of the 16th cleared, Lee's artillerists caught sight of Federal guns on the high bank beyond Antietam Creek. The thunder of a prolonged duel between Lee's guns and Brig. Gen. Henry Hunt's powerful Federal batteries soon rolled through the hills. There was no question in McClellan's mind now that Lee intended to hold Sharpsburg Ridge.

In midafternoon of the 16th, McClellan prepared for battle. Maj. Gen. Joseph Hooker's I Corps was instructed to take position opposite the Confederate left on the Hagerstown Pike. Maj. Gen. Joseph Mansfield's XII Corps and Maj. Gen. Edwin Sumner's II Corps were to extend the battleline from Hooker's left to the Smoketown Road and on to Antietam Creek near Pry's Mill Ford. The V Corps, Maj. Gen. Fitz-John Porter commanding, was directed to occupy the center of the Federal line on the Boonsboro Pike.

Burnside was to place his IX Corps just east of the Lower Bridge over Antietam Creek. Maj. Gen. William Franklin's VI Corps was to support the entire front. In the center, on the high east bank of Antietam Creek, and south of the Boonsboro Pike, General Hunt placed four batteries of 20-pounder Parrott rifles, the most powerful cannon on the field.

McClellan's plan called for an initial attack on the Confederate left flank on the Hagerstown Pike with the two corps of Hooker and Mansfield. McClellan intended to support this mass charge with Sumner's entire force and, if necessary, with Franklin's corps. If the powerful thrust against the Confederate left should succeed, McClellan would send Burnside's corps across Antietam Creek at the Lower Bridge and strike the Confederate right flank on the ridge southeast of Sharpsburg. Should Burnside succeed in turning the southern end of Lee's line, he would be expected to carry the attack northwest toward Sharpsburg. Finally, if either of these flanking movements appeared successful, McClellan would drive up the Boonsboro Pike with all available forces to smash the Confederate center.

It was a good plan. If the Federal attacks could be delivered in concert, McClellan's preponderance of power must stretch Lee's smaller force to the breaking point. But the story of Antietam is one of piecemeal Federal attacks—a corps here, a division there. This failure in execution allowed Lee to shift troops from momentarily quiet sectors to plug the gaps torn by the succession of Federal attacks. As each threat developed, Lee rushed his troops there and beat it back. Taking advantage of his interior lines, he re-

Meadow just beyond trees bordering Antietam Creek marks top of bluffs where many of Hunt's Union batteries were placed. This view from one-half mile in front of Confederate gun emplacements on Sharpsburg Ridge.

Brig. Gen. W. N. Pendleton, Lee's chief of artillery. From Miller's Photographic History of the Civil War.

Brig. Gen. Henry Hunt, McClellan's chief of artillery.

peatedly achieved a local advantage of numbers, though larger Federal contingents were always nearby.

The Lines Are Poised for Action

At 2 p.m. on the 16th, Hooker marched from his camp near Keedysville, crossed the Upper Bridge, and late in the afternoon reached the Hagerstown Pike. Under cover of the North Woods, his divisions formed for the attack on both sides of the pike. A massed force of more than 12,000 men was ready to advance on the Confederates.

Lee's thin line, 3 miles long, had been reinforced early on the 16th by the arrival of Jackson's troops from Harpers Ferry. They were placed where they could support the northern part of the

Union artillery in battery line. From 1863 photograph. Courtesy, Library of Congress.

Confederate line. John Walker's division, arriving from Harpers Ferry in the afternoon, took position south of Sharpsburg.

Jackson now commanded the Confederate front north of Sharpsburg; Longstreet, with a part of his force north of the village, extended the line nearly a mile south.

When Lee's outposts near Antietam Creek informed him in mid-afternoon that Hooker's Federals were massing north of Sharpsburg, Lee moved some of his men to advance positions. Hood established a line east of the Hagerstown Pike, with part of his troops in a cornfield and others extending the front to the East Woods. Skirmishers spread out far in front. Additional troops were rushed from reserve near Lee's headquarters at the Oak Grove west of Sharpsburg; they extended the line west across the Hagerstown Pike.

It was dusk by the time Hooker's force was ready to charge. With Maj. Gen. George Meade's men leading the way, they struck Hood's Confederates at the edge of the East Woods and in the adjacent fields. A brisk artillery fire from opposing batteries forced the men to seek cover. The gathering darkness made it difficult for the forces on either side to locate their marks. Gradually the opening skirmish at Antietam ended. The thrust of the Federal skirmishers, however, made it clear to Lee just where the next Federal blow would fall.

Even as Hooker's Federals withdrew to the cover of the North

Brig. Gen. John B. Hood.

Maj. Gen. Joseph Hooker. From photograph by Brady or assistant. Courtesy, Library of Congress.

Woods, strong forces were moving to their aid—the two powerful corps under Mansfield and Sumner. Mansfield would lead the XII Corps across Antietam Creek about midnight and encamp 1½ miles northeast of Hooker. Sumner's II Corps would cross the Antietam at Pry's Mill Ford at 7:30 the next morning to lend additional support.

Lee, too, was counting on reinforcements. McLaws' division was expected to arrive on the field by midmorning. A. P. Hill, who had been left at Harpers Ferry to handle details of the surrender, would arrive late in the day.

On the evening of September 16, picket lines were so close that the men on both sides, though unable to see each other, could hear footsteps. They knew that a tremendous struggle would begin at dawn. Some tried to sleep, but scattered firing throughout the night made this difficult. Others cleaned and cleaned again their rifled muskets, whose huge bullets made holes as big as silver dollars. Artillerists brought up ammunition for their smooth-bore Napoleons—so deadly at close range—and for the long-range rifled Parrott guns. And so these men got through the night, each one facing the impending crisis in his own way.

Union signal station on Elk Ridge. From here, McClellan's observers spotted Confederate troop movements during the battle. Courtesy, National Archives.

Hooker Strikes at Daybreak

A drizzling rain fell during the night. The morning of the 17th broke gray and misty, but the skies cleared early. As rays of light outlined the fringe of trees about the Dunkard Church, restless Federal skirmishers opened fire. A line of rifle fire flashed from the Southern muskets far out in front of the church. Soon, powerful Federal guns on the bluffs beyond Antietam Creek poured a raking fire of shot and shell into the Confederate lines. The first stage of McClellan's plan of crushing Lee—folding up the Confederate left flank—was about to begin.

Hooker struck with tremendous force. With skirmishers still hotly engaged, 10 brigades moved out from the cover of the North Woods. Brig. Gen. Abner Doubleday's men advanced along the Hagerstown Pike. Brig. Gen. James Ricketts' force charged down the Smoketown road toward the Dunkard Church. Part of Meade's division in the center was held in reserve. Hooker's artillery, massed on the ridge near the Poffenberger house, raked the Confederate lines. Heads down and bent to the side, like people breasting a hailstorm, the wave of Federals charged southward, spreading over the front from East Woods to the fringe of West Woods.

From left and from right, Confederate brigades poured into the fray to buttress Jackson's line of battle. D. H. Hill sent three brigades from the Sunken Road, dangerously weakening his own line—but then, first things first, and this is the story of the Confederate defense throughout the day. Hood's two brigades stood in reserve in the woods adjoining the Dunkard Church. Eight thousand Confederates awaited Hooker's assault.

While most of Jackson's men formed a line from east to west in front of the Dunkard Church, Brig. Gen. A. R. Lawton had sent a strong force into the Miller cornfield, 300 yards in advance, concealed, he believed, from the enemy.

East Woods on left; Miller cornfield, where Lawton's men were hidden, on right. This view looking south, as Hooker's men saw it at dawn.

View from the south, as Jackson's men saw it. Cornfield ahead; East Woods at right.

Doubleday's Federals came upon the cornfield. "As we appeared at the edge of the corn," related Maj. Rufus Dawes, "a long line of men in butternut and gray rose up from the ground. Simultaneously, the hostile battle lines opened a tremendous fire upon each other. Men, I cannot say fell; they were knocked out of the ranks by dozens." Hooker, nearby, saw farther in the field the reflection of sunlight from the enemy's bayonets projecting above the corn. Ordering all of his spare batteries to the left of this field, the Federal guns at close range raked the cornfield with canister and shell. "In the time I am writing," Hooker later wrote, "every stalk of corn in the northern and greater part of the field was cut as closely as could have been done with a knife, and the slain lay in rows precisely as they had stood in their ranks a few moments before. It was never my fortune to witness a more bloody, dismal battlefield."

Those Confederates who survived the slaughter in the cornfield now fled before the Federal onslaught. Heading for West Woods, they had to clamber over the picket-and-rail fence bordering the Hagerstown Pike; many were shot in the attempt and lay spread-eagled across the fence or piled on either side.

One soldier recalled the hysterical excitement that now gripped the Union troops: The only thought was victory. Without regard for safety, they charged forward, loading, firing, and shouting as they advanced. In contrast were the fallen—as waves of blue-clad troops swept by, wounded men looked up and cried for aid, but there was no time to stop.

Cornfield Avenue, marking southern limit of "bloody cornfield." Federals charged from right; Confederates counterattacked from left. From photograph taken on anniversary of battle, showing corn as it stood when the fighting began.

While Doubleday's division charged through the cornfield, Rickett's men, on the left of the attacking columns, pushed through the East Woods to its southern fringe. Capt. Dunbar Ransom's battery broke from the cover of the East Woods and fired shot and shell into the staggering Confederate lines.

For more than an hour, the battlefront flamed along an extended semicircular line from the open fields of the Mumma farm northwest through the cornfield to the rocky ledges in West Woods. The fury of the Federal attack had carried Doubleday's and Ricketts' men deep into the Confederate line, and now Meade's reserve brigades rushed forward.

In this critical stage, Jackson launched a driving counterattack. Hood's men, supported by D. H. Hill's brigades, battered the Federals back to the cornfield but were halted by the pointblank fire of Union guns in East Woods.

Mansfield Renews the Attack

As the remnants of Hooker's command sought shelter under the cover of powerful Federal batteries in front of East Woods, a new threat faced the Confederates. Mansfield's XII Corps, which had encamped more than a mile to the rear of Hooker during the night, had marched at the sound of Hooker's opening guns. At 7:30 a.m., almost an hour and a half later, Mansfield's force was approaching from the north in heavy columns.

Seeing Hooker's plight, Mansfield now rushed to the forefront of his men, urging them to the attack. But his work was cut short by a Confederate ball; mortally wounded, he was carried from the field.

Without pause, Brig. Gen. Alpheus Williams moved up to command and the attack swept on over ground just vacated by Hooker. On the right, Brig. Gen. Samuel Crawford's division bore down the Hagerstown Pike toward the Confederates in West Woods. Attacking in separate units, however, their lines were shattered by Brig. Gen. J. R. Jones' men, fighting from the cover of projecting rocks. J. E. B. Stuart's artillery, from the hill a half mile to the west, rapidly dispersed the remnants.

On the left, the Federals fared better. They pounded Hood's men back across the fields toward the Dunkard Church and opened a great gap in the Confederate line. Into the hole plunged Brig. Gen. George S. Greene's Union division. Only a desperate Confederate stand stopped Greene's men at the Dunkard Church. There they remained, an isolated salient beyond support—the Federal assault had shot its bolt.

Attacking separately, the two corps of Hooker and Mansfield had each come within a hair of breaking Jackson's line. What if they had attacked together? Again and again through this long day, the same question—changing only the names—would apply.

Taken back of the picket-and-rail fence on the Hagerstown Pike, where Jackson's men attempted to rally in the face of Hooker's charge. From photograph by Alexander Gardner. Courtesy, National Archives.

Maj. Gen. Joseph Mansfield.
Courtesy, Library of Congress.

It may have been while observing this critical fight near the Dunkard Church, that General Lee saw a straggler heading back toward camp lugging a pig that he had killed. With disaster so close, and straggling one of its chief causes, Lee momentarily lost control and ordered Jackson to shoot the man as an example to the army. Instead, Jackson gave the culprit a musket and placed him where action was hottest for the rest of the day. He came through unscathed and was afterward known as the man who had lost his pig but saved his bacon.

Jackson Prepares an Ambush

By 9 a.m., 3 hours of killing had passed. The Miller cornfield had become a no-mans' land, its tall stalks trampled to the ground

Going into Action. From etching by W. H. Shelton. Courtesy, Library of Congress.

and strewn with blood-soaked corpses. Firing had been so intense, had so fouled the men's muskets, that some of them were using rocks to pound their ramrods home.

For a moment, the fighting ceased. Then powerful reserves were rushed forward by commanders of both armies to renew the battle.

Jackson was in extreme danger. Green's Federals still lurked near the Dunkard Church, waiting only for support to renew their attack on the frayed Confederate line. And at this very moment a mass of blue-clad infantry could be seen emerging from the East Woods half a mile away—it was part of Sumner's II Corps moving up for the morning's third major Federal attack.

Swiftly Jackson gathered together reinforcements from other sectors of the battlefield. Some had just arrived from Harpers Ferry; these were McLaws' men. With hardly a pause they moved north and disappeared into the West Woods. Lee ordered Walker's two brigades north from the Lower Bridge; they too disappeared into the West Woods. Thus they came, racing from far and near.

As soon as they came in, Jackson craftily placed these men behind the rocks and ridges at the western fringe of the woods. Soon they formed a great semicircle whose outer points perfectly encompassed the 5,000 men in Sumner's approaching column. Ten-thousand Confederates were there. Now they disappeared into the landscape and waited.

Sumner's II Corps, under orders to support the attack on the Confederate left, had prepared at dawn to cross Antietam Creek at Pry's Mill Ford. Impatiently, Sumner had awaited the signal to march while the battle raged with increasing violence on the ridge beyond the stream. Finally, at 7:30 a.m., he led Maj. Gen. John

Knap's Independent Pennsylvania Battery "E" supported Mansfield's corps. Courtesy, National Archives.

Closeup of Dunkard Church where Greene's men were halted. From Gardner's Photographic Sketch Book. Courtesy, Library of Congress.

Federal artillery at Antietam. Note the observer in foreground, and the smoke of battle. From photograph by Alexander Gardner. Courtesy, Library of Congress.

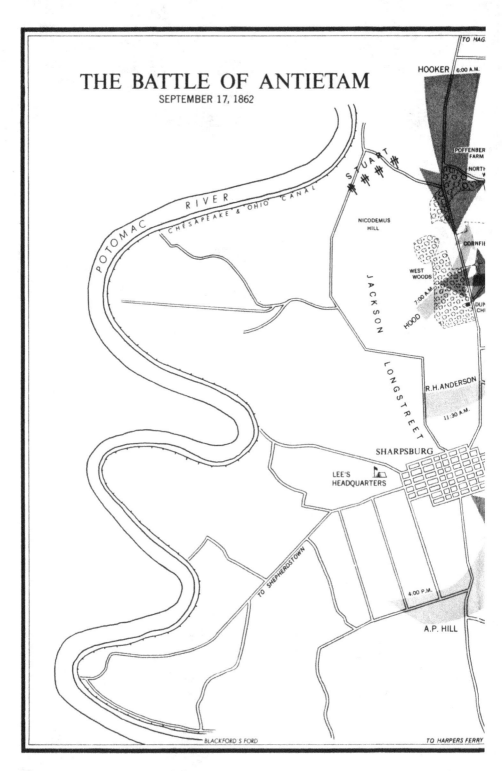

THE BATTLE OF ANTIETAM
SEPTEMBER 17, 1862

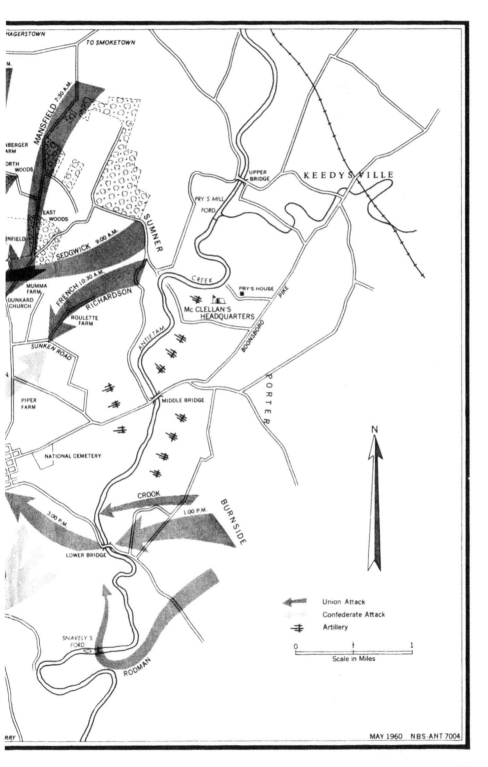

HAGERSTOWN
TO SMOKETOWN
M.
MANSFIELD 7:30 A.M.
BERGER FARM
ORTH WOODS
EAST WOODS
INFIELD
SEDGWICK 9:00 A.M.
SUMNER
FRENCH 10:30 A.M.
RICHARDSON
MUMMA FARM
DUNKARD CHURCH
ROULETTE FARM
SUNKEN ROAD
PIPER FARM
CREEK
ANTIETAM
PRY'S MILL FORD
UPPER BRIDGE
KEEDYSVILLE
PRY'S HOUSE
McCLELLAN'S HEADQUARTERS
BOONSBORO PIKE
MIDDLE BRIDGE
PORTER
NATIONAL CEMETERY
N
CROOK
1:00 P.M.
3:00 P.M.
BURNSIDE
LOWER BRIDGE
SNAVELY'S FORD
RODMAN
RRY

Union Attack
Confederate Attack
⚏ Artillery

0   1
Scale in Miles

MAY 1960   NBS-ANT 7004

29

Maj. Gen. Edwin V. Sumner. From photograph by Brady or assistant. Courtesy, Library of Congress.

Maj. Gen. John Sedgwick.

Sedgwick's division across the ford. Brig. Gen. William French's division followed, but soon drifted to the south and lost contact with Sedgwick.

Believing that he still led two divisions, Sumner continued his march past the East Woods. By now he knew that the earlier Federal attackers could give him no support, but he believed that the Confederates who had repulsed them must be equally exhausted and disorganized. Striking now—immediately—he might turn the tide before the enemy had time to recover. In his hurry, Sumner neglected to make sure that French's division followed closely in his rear. Neither had he taken time to reconnoiter the Confederate front in the West Woods.

Soon after 9 a.m., Sedgwick's heavy column, with Sumner at the head, started toward the Hagerstown Pike. Battleflags waving, bayonets glistening, the division marched forward in brigade front— long swaying lines of two ranks each.

Unmolested, they crossed the pike and passed into the West Woods. Almost surrounding them were Jackson's quietly waiting 10,000. Suddenly the trap was sprung. Caught within a pocket of almost encircling fire, in such compact formation that return fire was impossible, Sedgwick's men were reduced to utter helplessness. Completely at the mercy of the Confederates on the front, flank, and rear, the Federal lines were shattered by converging volleys. So appalling was the slaughter, nearly half of Sedgwick's 5,000 men, were struck down in less than 20 minutes.

The Halt of the Line of Battle. From the wartime sketch by Edwin Forbes. Courtesy, Library of Congress.

Scene of the ambush. Sedgwick's men marched in from left; note rock outcroppings where Jackson's men were hidden.

Part of the ground over which Sedgwick's men fought, possibly near Hagerstown Pike. Courtesy, National Archives.

But the trap had not been completely closed. In the confusion of the surprise assault, many regiments on the Federal right found an opening. Hastily withdrawing to the northeast, they soon found cover under the protecting fire of Sedgwick's artillery in the cornfield. Other batteries in the East Woods and to the north joined in the cannonade.

Eagerly grasping the opportunity for a counterattack, Jackson's line now swept across the open fields and charged the Federal batteries in front of East Woods. But the fire was more than sheer valor could overcome. Blasted with grape and canister from the crossfire of 50 guns, the Confederates staggered, then gave way and drew back to the cover of West Woods. There, protruding rock strata protected them. Meanwhile, from his menacing position near the Dunkard Church, Greene was driven back by Confederate reserves.

Three-quarters of Lee's army was now north of Sharpsburg. The successive Federal attacks had punched the northeast salient of the Confederate left and center inward toward the Dunkard Church. Now these two sectors were merged into one long line that ran roughly southeast from Nicodemus Hill, past the Dunkard Church, to end along the Sunken Road. What had been the right (southern)

Sunken Road in 1877.
The same view today.

Maj. Gen. Lafayette McLaws, who led Jackson's counterattack after the ambush. Courtesy, Frederick Hill Meserve Collection.

Maj. Gen. D. H. Hill. Courtesy, Library of Congress.

end of the long Confederate line was now the rear. Properly speaking, Lee had no center. He had two separate lines—the main one, facing northeast toward East Woods; and a detached guard force, facing southeast toward the Lower Bridge. Between them was only a thin line of riflemen. If McClellan now delivered simultaneous hammer blows from northeast, east, and southeast, he would surely destroy Lee's weak defensive setup. But if he continued his piece-meal attacks, Lee could keep on shuttling his brigades back and forth to meet them. And this is what they both did.

The Fight for the Sunken Road

Sedgwick may have wondered, in the moments before the Confederate onslaught in the West Woods, why General French was not closely following him. Nor is it clear, in view of French's instructions, why he did not do so.

French's troops had crossed Pry's Mill Ford in Sedgwick's wake. After marching about a mile west, they had veered south toward the Roulette farmhouse, possibly drawn that way by the fire of enemy skirmishers. Continuing to advance, they became engaged with Confederate infantry at the farmhouse and in a ravine which inclines southward to a ridge. On the crest of this ridge, a strong enemy force waited in a deeply cut lane—the Sunken Road.

Mumma farm, left; Roulette farmhouse, far right. This view looking east from Hagerstown Pike. French's division advanced from left toward the Sunken Road, which is off picture to the right. Both farmhouses seen in this modern view were here at time of the battle.

Worn down by farm use and the wash of heavy rains, this natural trench joins the Hagerstown Pike 500 yards south of the Dunkard Church. From this point the road runs east about 1,000 yards, then turns south toward the Boonsboro Pike. That first 1,000 yards was soon to be known as Bloody Lane.

Posted in the road embankment were the five brigades of D. H. Hill. At dawn these men had faced east, their line crossing the Sunken Road. But under the pressure of the Federal attacks on the Confederate left, they had swung northward. Three of Hill's brigades had been drawn into the fight around the Dunkard Church. Then Greene's Federals had driven them back toward the Sunken Road. There Hill rallied his troops. About 10:30 a.m., as the men were piling fence rails on the embankment to strengthen the position, a strong enemy force appeared on their front, steadily advancing with parade-like precision. It was French's division, heading up the ravine toward Sunken Road Ridge.

Crouched at the road embankment, Hill's men delivered a galling fire into French's ranks. The Federals fell back, then charged again. One Union officer later wrote: "For three hours and thirty minutes the battle raged incessantly, without either party giving way."

But French's division alone could not maintain its hold on the ridge. Hurt by fire from Confederates in the road and on either side, the Union men gave way. Still it was not over. French's reserve brigade now rushed up, restoring order in the disorganized ranks; once again the division moved forward.

Now, opportunely, Maj. Gen. Israel Richardson's Federal division—also of Sumner's corps—arrived on the left of French and was about to strike Hill's right flank in the road embankment.

It was a critical moment for the Confederates. Aware that loss of the Sunken Road might bring disaster, Lee ordered forward his last reserve—the five brigades of Maj. Gen. R. H. Anderson's division. At the same time Brig. Gen. Robert Rodes of Hill's division launched a furious attack to hold the Federals back until Anderson's men could arrive. This thrust kept French's men from aiding Richardson, who even now prepared to assault the Confederates in the road.

As French's attack halted, Richardson swept forward in magnificent array. Richardson was a tough old fighter—bluff and courageous, a leader of men. One of his officers recalled his leading the advance, sword in hand: "Where's General ————?" he cried. Some soldiers answered, "Behind the haystack!" "G-- d--- the field officers!" the old man roared, pushing on with his men toward the Sunken Road. In three units they passed to the east of the Roulette farmhouse and charged the Confederates at the crest of the ridge.

As the struggle increased in fury, R. H. Anderson's brigades arrived in the rear of Hill's troops in the road. But Anderson fell wounded soon after his arrival, and suddenly the charging Confederate counteroffensive lost its punch. By a mistaken order, Rodes' men in the Sunken Road near the Roulette lane withdrew to the rear. A dangerous gap opened on the Confederate front. The artillerist Lt. Col. E. P. Alexander wrote later, "When Rodes' brigade left the sunken road . . . Lee's army was ruined, and the end of the Confederacy was in sight."

Union Col. Francis Barlow saw the gap in the Confederate front opened by Rodes' withdrawal. Quickly swinging two regiments astride the road, he raked its length with perfectly timed volleys. Routed by this devastating enfilade, the Confederate defenders fled the road and retreated south toward Sharpsburg. Only a heroic rally by D. H. Hill's men prevented a breakthrough into the town.

The Sunken Road was now Bloody Lane. Dead Confederates lay so thick there, wrote one Federal soldier, that as far down the road as he could see, a man could have walked upon them without once touching ground.

The Federals had suffered heavily, too. Their bodies covered the

36

On the Firing Line. By Gilbert Gaul. Courtesy, Library of Congress.

Bloody Lane. Courtesy, Library of Congress.

approaches to the ridge. In the final moments, while leading his men in pursuit, Colonel Barlow had been seriously wounded; and shortly after, his commander, General Richardson, had fallen with a mortal wound.

The fight for the Sunken Road had exhausted both sides. At 1 p.m. they halted, and panting men grabbed their canteens to swish the dust and powder from their rasping throats.

The Confederate retreat from Bloody Lane had uncovered a great gap in the center of Lee's line. A final plunge through this hole would sever the Confederate army into two parts that could be destroyed in detail. "Only a few scattered handfuls of Harvey Hill's division were left," wrote Gen. William Allen, "and R. H. Anderson's was hopelessly confused and broken. . . . There was no body of Confederate infantry in this part of the field that could have resisted a serious advance." So desperate was the situation that General Longstreet himself held horses for his staff while they served two cannon supporting Hill's thin line.

But McClellan's caution stopped the breakthrough before it was born. Though Franklin's VI Corps was massed for attack, McClellan restrained it. "It would not be prudent to make the attack," he told Franklin after a brief examination of the situation, "our position on the right being . . . considerably in advance of what it had been in the morning."

So McClellan turned to defensive measures. Franklin's reserve corps would not be committed, but would remain in support of the Federal right. And in the center, McClellan held back Fitz-John Porter's V Corps. After all, reasoned the Federal commander, was not this the only force that stood between the enemy and the Federal supply train on the Boonsboro Pike?

But Porter was not quite alone. The entire Federal artillery reserve stood with him. Further, Brig. Gen. Alfred Pleasonton had placed his cavalry and artillery on a commanding ridge west of the Middle Bridge during the morning. From here he had already supported the attack by Sumner's corps on the Sunken Road, and he had aided Burnside's efforts on the left. Now he stood poised for further action. Pleasonton was to wait in vain. His dual purpose of obtaining ". . . an enfilading fire upon the enemy in front of Burnside, and of enabling Sumner to advance to Sharpsburg" was nullified by McClellan's decision to halt and take the defensive.

In striking contrast to McClellan's caution, General Lee was at that very moment considering a complete envelopment of the Federal flank at the North and East Woods. By this means he might relieve the pressure on D. H. Hill; for despite the lull, Lee could not believe that McClellan had halted the attack there. If the attack in the North Woods succeeded, Lee hoped to drive the Federal remnants to the banks of Antietam Creek and administer a crushing defeat.

Jackson and J. E. B. Stuart, early in the afternoon, shifted northward and prepared to charge the Federal lines. When they arrived close to the powerful Federal artillery on Poffenberger Ridge, they saw that a Confederate attack there would be shattered by these massed guns. A wholesome respect for Federal artillerists now forced Lee to withdraw his order. As he did so, heavy firing to the south heralded a new threat developing there.

Burnside Takes the Lower Bridge

During the morning of the 17th, Confederate observers on the ridge north of Sharpsburg had spotted masses of Federals moving southward beyond Antietam Creek. These were the four divisions of Burnside's IX Corps concentrating for the attack on the Lower Bridge.

Topography at the Lower Bridge heavily favored the few hundred Georgia men who defended it under the leadership of Brig. Gen. Robert Toombs. The road approaching the east end of the bridge swings on a course paralleling that of Antietam Creek; in the last few hundred yards before reaching the bridge, the road plunges into a funnel-like depression between the opposing bluffs of the creek. Toombs' men were in rifle pits on the west bluff overlooking the bridge and the approach road.

Because of faulty reconnaissance, Burnside did not know that fords were nearby where his men could have waded across the stream. Instead, the Federal plan of attack forced the advancing columns to pile into this funnel and storm across the bridge.

Soon after 9 a.m., the Federal divisions began to assault the bridge. One after another, their gallant charges were broken by deadly short-range fire from Toombs' Georgians. By noon, when the agony at the Sunken Road was reaching its highest pitch, and despite repeated orders from McClellan to get across Antietam Creek at all costs, the bottleneck at the bridge was still unbroken.

Meanwhile, Brig. Gen. Isaac Rodman's Union division had moved slowly downstream from the bridge in search of a crossing. Rounding a sharp bend in the creek, nearly a mile south, scouts came upon shallow water at Snavely's Ford. Late in the morning Rodman crossed the stream and began to drive against the right flank of the Georgians guarding the bridge. About the same time, Col. George Crook's scouts located a ford a few hundred yards above the bridge; there he sent his brigade across. Capt. Seth J. Simonds' battery was placed in position to command the bridge.

Maj. Gen. Ambrose E. Burnside. From photograph by Brady or assistant. Courtesy, Library of Congress.

Burnside or Lower Bridge shortly after the battle. Toombs' men were on the bluff in background. Courtesy, Library of Congress.

Burnside's men storm the bridge. From wartime sketch by Forbes.

The same view today. Note how tree at near end of bridge has grown.

Zouaves of Burnside's IX Corps charge toward Sharpsburg. From wartime sketch by Forbes. Courtesy, Library of Congress.

At 1 p.m., the defending Confederates saw a sudden stir across Antietam Creek. Two regiments, the 51st New York and the 51st Pennsylvania, marched swiftly out from the cover of the wooded hill and charged for the bridge. Supported now by converging artillery fire, they quickly formed into columns and were over the bridge before Confederate artillery could halt them. Soon a wide gap split the Confederate defense. Masses of Federal troops poured across the bridge while Rodman and Crook hammered the Confederate flanks. Burnside's men had gained the west bank of the creek.

But again there was fateful delay as Burnside paused to reorganize. By the time he was ready to drive the Southern defenders from the ridge in his front, 2 critical hours had passed.

Close to 3 p.m., the mighty Federal line moved slowly up the hill toward Sharpsburg, then gained momentum. "The movement of the dark column," related an observer, "with arms and banners glittering in the sun, following the double line of skirmishers, dashing forward at a trot, loading and firing alternately as they moved, was one of the most brilliant and exciting exhibitions of the day."

First brushing aside the depleted ranks in the rifle pits above the bridge, the Federals struck D. R. Jones' four lonely brigades on the hills southeast of Sharpsburg—whence every other Confederate infantry unit had been withdrawn to reinforce the line to the north. Unable to stem the massive Federal attack, Jones' men were driven back toward the town.

To halt the Federal tide, Lee shifted all available artillery south-

A Confederate battery on this site on the Harpers Ferry Road fired on Burnside's men as they charged toward the left across the low ground in the middle distance. A. P. Hill's division marched behind these guns, going left, then turned off the road and passed through the cornfield to hit Burnside's corps in flank.

ward. By 4 p.m., however, the Federals were approaching the village itself; only a half mile lay between them and Lee's line of retreat to the Potomac. Disaster seemed at hand for Lee's decimated force.

A. P. Hill Turns the Tide

But now came a great moment in Confederate military annals. A. P. Hill's notable Light Division, having hurriedly crossed the Potomac, 3 miles away, was driving hard toward the jubilant Federals charging on Sharpsburg. Some of Hill's artillery had already arrived from Harpers Ferry with the cheering news that Hill's brigades of infantry were close by.

At Lee's urgent order, Hill had left Harpers Ferry early. Sensing the critical role they would play, urged on at sword point by their grim commander, Hill's veterans had covered the 17 miles from Harpers Ferry to the Potomac in 7 hours. Hundreds of men had fallen out, unable to keep the pace. Now, across the river, the stalwart survivors pounded on toward the sound of the guns.

Suddenly the head of Hill's column appeared on the road to the south. Hill rode up to Lee's headquarters at the Oak Grove, then quickly to D. R. Jones, whose exhausted troops formed the last de-

Maj. Gen. A. P. Hill. From an engraving by A. H. Ritchie.

fense line in front of Sharpsburg. Hill's five brigades now rushed toward the Federal flank. Confusion gripped Burnside's men as this unexpected onslaught plowed into their lines. Men broke and started to run. In moments the tide had turned. The Federal lines, sagging from the overwhelming charge of the Southerners, and with gaping holes cut by artillery, fell back across the hills to the sheltering banks of Antietam Creek.

Powerful Federal artillery continued to thunder across the hills; heavy blue columns could still be seen in overmastering strength across Antietam Creek and far to the north. But the Federal commander had called a halt.

An hour and a half after the timely arrival of A. P. Hill's division from Harpers Ferry, the battle ended. With sunset, the firing died away. That night, the tired men lay on their arms in line of battle. Neither side would admit defeat; neither could claim the victory.

Retreat from Sharpsburg

Seldom had Lee's army fought a battle so strenuous and so long. "The sun," a soldier wrote, "seemed almost to go backwards, and it appeared as if night would never come." From dawn to sunset, the Confederate commander had thrown into battle every organized unit north of the Potomac. Straggling in the days preceding Antietam had reduced Lee's army from 55,000 to 41,000 men. This small force had sustained five major attacks by McClellan's 87,000-

Blackford's Ford from the Maryland side of the Potomac.

man army—three in the West Woods and the Miller cornfield, and those at the Sunken Road and the Lower Bridge—each time the outcome hanging in the balance.

In the stillness of the night, Lee called his commanders to his headquarters west of Sharpsburg. Of each in turn he asked the condition of the men, and each, even Jackson, spoke against renewal of battle on the morrow. "Still too weak to assume the offensive," Lee wrote later, "we waited without apprehension the renewal of the attack."

Early on the following morning, it became apparent that McClellan was not going to attack, though during the night he had received strong reinforcements, and more were on the way. Still undaunted, Lee returned to his plan of striking the Federal right at Poffenberger Ridge. But after surveying the ground, his officers informed him that Federal batteries completely dominated the narrow strip of land over which the attack must be launched. An attempt against the Federal guns would be suicidal.

Balked in his last hope of a counteroffensive, Lee realized that he could not recall the decision won by McClellan at South Mountain: The campaign was lost. During the afternoon, he announced to his lieutenants his intention of withdrawing that night across the Potomac. At midnight Longstreet led the way across Blackford's Ford and formed a protective line on the south bank. Steadily through the night and early morning, the Confederate columns crossed over into Virginia.

McClellan did not actively pursue. As the days passed and Lee's army withdrew into the Shenandoah Valley, President Lincoln became impatient. The time was at hand, he thought, for the decisive blow. Calling upon McClellan on the field of Antietam, October 1, Lincoln urged a vigorous pursuit of the Confederate army. McClellan insisted that his army required reorganization and new equipment. The President, having lost all confidence in McClellan, removed him from command on November 7.

The Battle and the Campaign

Tactically, Antietam was a draw. Strategically, however, it was a Northern victory because it halted Lee's invasion.

Though McClellan failed to destroy Lee's army, his contribution was in many ways notable. In the 3 weeks after he was chosen for command on September 3, he provided for Washington's defense, created a new field army, fought two major actions, compelled Lee's evacuation of Maryland, and established Federal control of the Potomac River from Washington to Williamsport. That he was not a daring commander of Lee's stripe cannot detract from these solid achievements.

Lee, on the other hand, may have been too daring. Because of this he made two major miscalculations. First, his invasion of Maryland imposed a strain that his poorly equipped and exhausted army could not support; heavy straggling was the surest evidence of this. Second, he misjudged the capacity of the enemy to recuperate from the effects of Second Manassas and quickly put a reliable field army on his trail. He did achieve one of his objectives: The delay of the Federal armies in resuming major offensive operations in Virginia until the next winter. But the price was high and the South could not afford the kind of attrition suffered in the campaign.

Casualties were so heavy in the Battle of Antietam that September 17, 1862, is termed the bloodiest day of the Civil War. Of McClellan's 26,023 killed, wounded, and captured during the Maryland Campaign (including Harpers Ferry), he counted 12,410 at Antietam. Of Lee's 13,385 casualties during the campaign, 10,700 fell at Antietam.

The War for the Union Takes on a New Purpose

After Antietam there was no serious threat of foreign recognition or intervention on behalf of the Confederacy. And the repulse inflicted on Lee's Army of Northern Virginia gave Abraham Lincoln

Lincoln visits McClellan and his staff after the battle. McClellan is the fourth man to the left from the President. Courtesy, National Archives.

Lincoln and McClellan confer on the field of Antietam.

The President reads the Emancipation Proclamation to his cabinet. From an engraving based on the painting by Francis Bicknell Carpenter. Courtesy, Library of Congress.

the opportunity he had sought: On September 22—just 5 days after the battle—the President issued the preliminary Emancipation Proclamation. It declared that upon the first day of January next all slaves within any State or district then in rebellion against the United States ". . . shall be then, thenceforward, and forever free."

With the formal Emancipation Proclamation of January 1, 1863, the war took on new purpose. In the North, and in many foreign lands, the cause of American Union had become one with that of human liberty.

Clara Barton at Antietam

At Antietam, also, was Clara Barton, founder of the American Red Cross. On this field of desolation, long after the guns had ceased, Miss Barton was still busily rendering care to the wounded and dying. Having arrived early in the day in the northern area of battle, she witnessed the wounded men of Sedgwick's depleted ranks streaming to the cover of North and East Woods. By midmorning her

Barn near Keedysville, used as field hospital after the battle. Courtesy, National Archives.

wagonload of supplies, donated by the citizens of Washington, had arrived. She worked tirelessly with army surgeons at the field hospital on the Joseph Poffenberger farm. Her supply of bandages, linens, anesthetics, and oil lanterns replenished the surgeons' urgent need of dressings and provided light to carry on through the night. So outstanding were her services on the field of battle that she later received official recognition by the United States Army Medical Corps. Her work here and later would become basic to the establishment of the American Red Cross.

Antietam National Battlefield Site and Cemetery

Antietam National Battlefield Site was established August 30, 1890, to commemorate the significant events of September 17, 1862, and to preserve the important features of the battlefield. Administered by the War Department until 1933, the site was transferred that year to the U.S. Department of the Interior to be administered by the National Park Service.

Clara Barton. Courtesy, Library of Congress.

Citizen volunteers assisting the wounded at Antietam. From wartime sketch by Waud. Courtesy, Library of Congress.

Maryland Monument.

Turner's Gap looking east.

War Correspondents Memorial Arch Crampton's Gap.

The Battle of Antietam was fought over an area of 12 square miles. The site today consists of 184 acres containing approximately 5 miles of paved avenues. Located along the battlefield avenues to mark battle positions of infantry, artillery, and cavalry are many monuments, markers, and narrative tablets. Similar markers describe the actions at Turner's Gap, Harpers Ferry, and Blackford's Ford.

Lee headquarters marker in the Oak Grove.

Key artillery positions on the field of Antietam are marked by cannon. And 10 large-scale field exhibits at important points on the field indicate troop positions and battle action.

The War Correspondents' Memorial Arch and the 1st New Jersey Regimental Monument are located at Crampton's Gap, and at Fox's Gap is the memorial to Maj. Gen. Jesse Reno, who was killed while leading the Federal attack there.

Outstanding in the observance of battle anniversaries at Antietam was the occasion of the 75th anniversary on September 17, 1937. Thirty-five thousand persons, including 50 veterans who fought at Antietam, joined in the observance held on the battleground near the Sunken Road.

The Robert E. Lee Memorial tablet, located in a plot at the

The National Cemetery.

McClellan's headquarters, the Philip Pry House.

western limits of Sharpsburg, marks the headquarters of General Lee. General McClellan's headquarters were in the Philip Pry house, 2 miles east of Sharpsburg near the Boonsboro Pike.

The National Cemetery, located at the eastern limits of Sharpsburg, is the burial place of Federal dead from the Battles of Antietam, South Mountain, and minor engagements. The cemetery was established by an act of the Maryland legislature in March 1865; the dedication took place September 17, 1867, the fifth anniversary of the battle. The cemetery plot of 11 acres was deeded by the State of Maryland to the United States Government on March 13, 1878. Of 4,773 Civil War burials, 1,836 are listed as unidentified. The total number of burials, including nearly 300 from recent wars, is more than 5,000.

Administration

Antietam National Battlefield Site is a part of the National Park System, owned by the people of the United States and administered for them by the National Park Service, U.S. Department of the Interior. Communications should be addressed to the Superintendent, Antietam National Battlefield Site, Sharpsburg, Md.

Suggested Readings

BRADFORD, NED, editor, *Battles and Leaders of the Civil War.* Appleton-Century-Crofts, New York, 1956.

These selections from the original four volume 1887–88 edition are excellent for on-the-spot impressions of participants. Should be used with caution concerning historical accuracy.

CATTON, BRUCE, *Mr. Lincoln's Army.* Doubleday & Company, Garden City, 1951.

Popular well-written interpretive study with colorful battle accounts. Descriptions of camplife are very good.

COMMAGER, HENRY S., editor, *The Blue and the Gray.* Bobbs-Merrill Company, Inc., New York, 1950.

Fine selection of readings from the pens of participants. Again, as with *Battles and Leaders,* these accounts suffer from immediacy and should be used with caution.

FREEMAN, D. S., *R. E. Lee,* Vol. II. Charles Scribner's Sons, New York, 1934.

Outstanding as biography and as military history. Detailed analysis of Lee's actions as commander with vivid battle descriptions. Excellent footnotes for further reference.

HASSLER, WARREN W., JR., *General George B. McClellan, Shield of the Union.* Louisiana State University Press, Baton Rouge, 1957.

Interesting interpretation of McClellan's actions as Federal commander. His difficulties with subordinates, especially Burnside, are used to explain Federal failure to take advantage of opportunities at Antietam.

HENDERSON, G. F. R., *Stonewall Jackson and the American Civil War.* Longmans, Green and Company, London, 1955 reprint.

This is a modern reprint of Henderson's classic military biography, first printed in 1898; it is still a standard work on the legendary Jackson.

LONGSTREET, JAMES, *From Manassas to Appomattox.* J. B. Lippincott and Company, Philadelphia, 1896.

Written many years after the war, this account by a leading participant emphasizes his own point of view.

APPENDIX

The Emancipation Proclamation

On August 22, 1862, just one month before Abraham Lincoln issued the preliminary Emancipation Proclamation, he wrote a letter to Horace Greeley, abolitionist editor of the New York Tribune.. The letter read in part:

I would save the Union. I would save it the shortest way under the Constitution. The sooner the National authority can be restored, the nearer the Union will be "the Union as it was." If there be those who would not save the Union unless they could at the same time *save* Slavery, I do not agree with them. If there be those who would not save the Union unless they could at the same time *destroy* Slavery, I do not agree with them. My paramount object in this struggle *is* to save the Union, and is *not* either to save or destroy Slavery. . . . I have here stated my purpose according to my view of official duty, and I intend no modification of my oft-expressed personal wish that all men everywhere could be free. . . .

For some months before the Battle of Antietam, as his letter to Greeley indicates, Lincoln had been wrestling with the problem of slavery and its connection with the war. He became convinced that a new spiritual and moral force—emancipation of the slaves—must be injected into the Union cause, else the travail of war might dampen the fighting spirit of the North. If this loss of vitality should come to pass, the paramount political objective of restoring the Union might never be attained.

Another compelling factor in Lincoln's thinking was the need to veer European opinion away from its sympathy for the South. A war to free the slaves would enlist the support of Europe in a way that a war for purely political objectives could not.

Thus, slowly and with much soul searching, Lincoln's official view of his duty came to correspond with his personal wish for human freedom. The outcome of these deliberations was the Emancipation Proclamation.

The Federal victory at Antietam gave Lincoln the opportunity to issue the proclamation—a dramatic step toward eliminating slavery in the United States.

By this act, Lincoln stretched the Constitution to the limit of its meaning. His interpretation of presidential war powers was revolutionary. It would become a precedent for other Presidents who would similarly find constitutional authority for emergency action in time of war.

By the "President of the United States of America:

A Proclamation.

Whereas, on the twentysecond day of September, in the year of our Lord one thousand eight hundred and sixtytwo, a proclamation was issued by the President of the United States, containing, among other things, the following, towit:

"That on the first day of January, in the year of our Lord one thousand eight hundred and sixty-three, all persons held as slaves within any State or designated part of a State, the people whereof shall then be in rebellion against the United States, shall be then, thenceforward, and forever free; and the Executive Government of the United States, including the military and naval authority thereof, will recognize and maintain the freedom of such persons, and will do no act or acts to repress such persons, or any of them, in any efforts they may make for their actual freedom.

"That the Executive will, on the first day of January aforesaid, by proclamation, designate the States and parts of States, if any, in which the people thereof, respectively, shall then be in rebellion against the United States; and the fact that any State, or the people thereof, shall on that day be, in good faith, represented in the Congress of the United States by members chosen thereto at elections wherein a majority of the qualified voters of such State shall have participated, shall, in the absence of strong countervailing testimony, be deemed conclusive evidence that such State, and the people thereof, are not then in rebellion against the United States."

Now, therefore I, Abraham Lincoln, President of the United States, by virtue of the power in me vested as Commander-in-Chief, of the Army and Navy of the United States in time of actual armed rebellion against authority and government of the United States, and as a fit and necessary war measure for suppressing said rebellion, do, on this first day of January, in the year of our Lord one thousand eight hundred and sixtythree, and in accordance with my purpose so to do, publicly proclaimed for the full period of one hundred days, from the day first above mentioned, order and designate

20820

First page of Lincoln's handwritten draft of the formal Emancipation Proclamation.
Courtesy, Library of Congress.

58

More important, the proclamation was to inaugurate a revolution in human relationships. Although Congress had previously enacted laws concerning the slaves that went substantially as far as the Emancipation Proclamation, the laws had lacked the dramatic and symbolic import of Lincoln's words. Dating from the proclamation, the war became a crusade and the vital force of abolition sentiment was captured for the Union cause, both at home and abroad—especially in England.

The immediate practical effects of the Emancipation Proclamation were negligible, applying as it did only to those areas "in rebellion" where it could not be enforced. But its message became a symbol and a goal which opened the way for universal emancipation in the future. Thus the Thirteenth, Fourteenth, and Fifteenth Amendments to the Constitution are direct progeny of Lincoln's proclamation.

Any document with the long-term importance of the Emancipation Proclamation deserves to be read by those who experience its effects. Following is the text of the formal Emancipation Proclamation, issued on January 1, 1863:

BY THE PRESIDENT OF THE UNITED STATES OF AMERICA:

A Proclamation.

WHEREAS on the 22d day of September, A.D. 1862, a proclamation was issued by the President of the United States, containing, among other things, the following, to wit:

"That on the 1st day of January, A.D. 1863, all persons held as slaves within any State or designated part of a State the people whereof shall then be in rebellion against the United States shall be then, thenceforward, and forever free; and the executive government of the United States, including the military and naval authority thereof, will recognize and maintain the freedom of such persons and will do no act or acts to repress such persons, or any of them, in any efforts they may make for their actual freedom.

"That the executive will on the 1st day of January aforesaid, by proclamation, designate the States and parts of States, if any, in which the people thereof, respectively, shall then be in rebellion against the United States; and the fact that any State or the people thereof shall on that day be in good faith represented in the Congress of the United States by members chosen thereto at elections wherein a majority of the qualified voters of such States shall have participated shall, in the absence of strong countervailing testimony, be deemed conclusive evidence that such State and the people thereof are not then in rebellion against the United States."

Now, therefore, I, Abraham Lincoln, President of the United States, by virtue of the power in me vested as Commander-in-Chief of the Army and Navy of the United States in time of actual armed rebellion against the authority and government of the United States, and as a fit and necessary war measure for suppressing said rebellion, do, on this 1st day of January, A.D. 1863, and in accordance with my purpose so to do, publicly proclaimed for the full period of one hundred days from the first day above mentioned, order and designate as the States and parts of States wherein the people thereof, respectively, are this day in rebellion against the United States the following, to wit:

Arkansas, Texas, Louisiana (except the parishes of St. Bernard, Paquemines, Jefferson, St. John, St. Charles, St. James, Ascension, Assumption, Terrebonne, Lafourche, St. Mary, St. Martin, and Orleans, including the city of New Orleans), Mississippi, Alabama, Florida, Georgia, South Carolina, North Carolina, and Virginia (except the forty-eight counties designated as West Virginia, and also the counties of Berkeley, Accomac, Northhampton, Elizabeth City, York, Princess Anne, and Norfolk, including the cities of Norfolk and Portsmouth), and which excepted parts are for the present left precisely as if this proclamation were not issued.

And by virtue of the power and for the purpose aforesaid, I do order and declare that all persons held as slaves within said designated States and parts of States are, and henceforward shall be, free; and that the Executive Government of the United States, including the military and naval authorities thereof will recognize and maintain the freedom of said persons.

And I hereby enjoin upon the people so declared to be free to abstain from all violence, unless in necessary self-defense; and I recommend to them that, in all cases when allowed, they labor faithfully for reasonable wages.

And I further declare and make known that such persons of suitable condition will be received into the armed service of the United States to garrison forts, positions, stations, and other places, and to man vessels of all sorts in said service.

And upon this act, sincerely believed to be an act of justice, warranted by the Constitution upon military necessity, I invoke the considerate judgement of mankind and the gracious favor of Almighty God.

U.S. GOVERNMENT PRINTING OFFICE : 1961 OF—595930

DSI's New Releases:
Civil War Battlefield Guides

ISBN	Title	Page Count	Price
1582187770	Manassas (Bull Run)	56	$8.95
1582187789	Chickamauga and Chattanooga Battlefields	72	$8.95
1582187800	Gettysburg National Military Park	60	$8.95
1582187819	Shiloh National Military Park, Tennessee	58	$8.95
1582187827	Antietam National Battlefield Site, Maryland	72	$8.95
1582187835	Petersburg National Military Park, Virginia	68	$8.95
1582187843	Fort Sumter National Monument, South Carolina	56	$8.95

To order visit:
www.PDFLibrary.com

CPSIA information can be obtained
at www.ICGtesting.com
Printed in the USA
BVHW061558070222
628203BV00002B/469

9 781582 187822